AFRICAN-AMERICAN COLLECTIVE BIOGRAPHIES

Awesome African-American Rock and Soul Musicians

David Aretha

Enslow Publishers, Inc.
40 Industrial Road
Box 398
Berkeley Heights, NJ 07922
USA

http://www.enslow.com

Library of Congress Cataloging-in-Publication Data

Aretha, David.
  Awesome African-American rock and soul musicians / David Aretha.
      p. cm. — (African-American collective biographies)
  Includes bibliographical references and index.
  Summary: "Read about important African-American musicians including: Chuck Berry,
Little Richard, James Brown, Ray Charles, Diana Ross, Aretha Franklin, Stevie Wonder,
Jimi Hendrix, and Prince"—Provided by publisher.
  ISBN 978-1-59845-140-5
  1. African-American rock musicians—Biography—Juvenile literature. 2. Soul musi-
cians—United States—Biography—Juvenile literature. I. Title.
  ML3929.A74 2012
  781.64089'96073—dc23

                    2011019956

Future editions:
Paperback ISBN 978-1-4644-0039-1
eBook ISBN 978-1-4645-0946-9
PDF ISBN 978-1-4646-0946-6

Printed in the United States of America

032012 Lake Book Manufacturing, Inc., Melrose Park, IL

10 9 8 7 6 5 4 3 2 1

To Our Readers: We have done our best to make sure all Internet addresses in this book
were active and appropriate when we went to press. However, the author and the publisher have no control over and assume no liability for the material available on those
Internet sites or on other Web sites they may link to. Any comments or suggestions can
be sent by e-mail to comments@enslow.com or to the address on the back cover.

♻ Enslow Publishers, Inc., is committed to printing our books on recycled paper. The
paper in every book contains 10% to 30% post-consumer waste (PCW). The cover board
on the outside of each book contains 100% PCW. Our goal is to do our part to help young
people and the environment too!

Illustration Credits: AP Images, pp. 5, 10, 92; AP Images: Charles Rex Arbogast, p. 53,
Dita Alangkara, p. 43, Evan Agostini, p. 82, Gary Null/NBC/NBCU Photo Bank, p. 12,
Jason DeCrow, p. 72, Mark Humphrey, p. 33, Paul W. Bailey/NBCU Photo Bank, p. 68,
Sipa, p. 22; Everett Collection, pp. 6, 9, 16, 30, 40, 50, 60; Photoshot/Courtesy Everett
Collection, p. 88; Rex Features/Courtesy Everett Collection, pp. 63, 78; © Universal/
Courtesy Everett Collection, p. 24.

Cover Illustration: Ray Stevenson/Rex Features/Courtesy Everett Collection

Contents

Introduction

For decades, the myth persisted that white musicians created rock 'n' roll in the mid-1950s. "Rock Around the Clock" (1955), by Bill Haley and His Comets, was credited as the breakthrough rock 'n' roll record. Elvis Presley, the "King of Rock 'n Roll," burst onto the scene with "Hound Dog" in 1956. Jerry Lee Lewis and Buddy Holly—two other white singers—electrified the late 1950s. However, most people didn't realize that rock 'n' roll had begun to evolve before the mid-1950s.

Much of rock 'n' roll was steeped in white musical styles such as country music and folk music. However, such African-American styles as gospel, boogie-woogie, blues, and rhythm and blues were even stronger influences. "The contribution of black artists to rock 'n' roll can't be overstated," said Tim Moore, communications director for the Rock and Roll Hall of Fame and Museum in Cleveland. "The music of the black church and the music of the blues are the bedrock of what became known as rock 'n' roll."[1]

African Americans Bo Diddley, Chuck Berry, and Little Richard were among the giants of early rock 'n' roll. But while they were successful in their day, audiences largely overlooked them in favor of white rockers. Little Richard's explosive 1955 recording "Tutti Frutti" rose to No. 17 on the pop music charts. But a year later, clean-cut white singer Pat Boone went to No. 12 with a tame cover version of that song. That year, Elvis took the nation by storm with "Hound Dog." But few knew that Big Mama Thornton, a black woman, had recorded the song three years earlier. The other big hit by Bill Haley and His Comets, "Shake, Rattle and Roll," was first recorded by Big Joe Turner.

Singer, composer, and pianist Fats Domino in 1956

Bo Diddley and his distinctive guitar in the 1950s

Introduction

Looking back on his idols, Beatles legend John Lennon said: "Berry is the greatest influence on earth. So is Bo Diddley, and so is Little Richard. There is not one white group on earth that hasn't got their music in them. And that's all I ever listened to. The only white person I ever listened to was Presley on his early music, and he was doing black music."[2] Black musicians also influenced the Rolling Stones. In fact, the band was named after the Muddy Waters song "Rollin' Stone."

The black roots of rock 'n' roll run deep. In such cities as New Orleans and Chicago in the early 1900s, African Americans played the blues in local clubs. Over time, musicians added rhythm to these sad songs to create livelier music. This genre, which came to be known as rhythm and blues, was called "race" (black) music in the 1930s and 1940s. It was great music, but white radio stations never played these black records. Many white listeners never got to hear songs such as "Rock and Roll Blues" (1949) by Erline Harris.

By the early 1950s, a few white disc jockeys began playing "race" records to multiracial radio audiences. Cleveland DJ Alan Freed introduced the term "rock 'n' roll" to the masses. In the 1956 film *Rock Rock Rock*, Freed declared: "Rock 'n' roll is a river of music, which has absorbed many streams: rhythm and blues, jazz, ragtime, cowboy songs, country songs, folk songs. All have contributed greatly to the Big Beat."[3]

A heavy guitar element and a strong backbeat (emphasis on the second and fourth beat of each four-beat measure) made rock 'n' roll distinctive. It was also played at a faster, more exciting pace, which young people loved. Said Little Richard, "Played up-tempo [fast], you call it rock 'n' roll; at a regular tempo, you call it rhythm and blues."[4]

Black musicians produced much of the great rock 'n' roll music of the 1950s. Many historians credit "Rocket 88," a 1951 song by African-American Jackie Brenston, as the first real rock 'n' roll hit. Other great early black rock 'n' rollers not featured in this book include:

❈ T–Bone Walker: pioneered the electric guitar sound in the 1930s

❈ Louis Jordan: a 1940s singer, saxophonist, and bandleader known as the "Father of Rhythm and Blues" and "Grandfather of Rock 'n' Roll"

❈ Muddy Waters: a blues legend who played a killer electric guitar

❈ Bo Diddley: an inventive musician whose strong rhythms and hard guitar sound helped lay the foundation for rock 'n' roll

❈ Fats Domino: a pianist, singer, and songwriter who sold 65 million records beginning in the 1950s

A Cry in Their Voices

By the early 1960s, African Americans' influence on rock 'n' roll began to fade. White rock bands from Great Britain began to dominate the music scene, a turn of events known as the British Invasion. Said Tim Moore: "I think what happened in the 1960s, with the advent of the Civil Rights Movement, blacks began to look down on blues as being too passive and rock 'n' roll as being too happy. So we moved on to a more soulful music, and left whites with rock music and the ability to define it as they pleased."[5]

Soul music is hard to define. "It's like electricity," said soul singer Ray Charles, "we don't really know what

Muddy Waters in the late 1940s or early 1950s

Gospel singer Mahalia Jackson, photographed on March 15, 1963

10

it is, but it's a force that can light a room."[6] In this genre, performers sing "from the soul." Their voices capture the pain, anguish, elation, and other strong emotions of the African-American experience.

Soul music has its roots in both blues and gospel music (passionate, Christian-themed music sung in black churches). Mahalia Jackson, a legendary gospel singer who emerged in the 1930s, traces soul music back to the days of slavery. It started,

Introduction

she said, with "the groans and moans of the people in the cotton fields. Before it got the name of soul, men were sellin' watermelons and vegetables on a wagon drawn by a mule, hollerin' 'watermellllon!' with a cry in their voices. And the men on the railroad track layin' crossties—every time they hit the hammer it was with a sad feelin', but with a beat."[7]

Soul singers James Brown, Ray Charles, and Aretha Franklin—the "Queen of Soul"—are profiled in this book. But so many others are worthy of mention. Here are but a few, along with their signature song:

❁ Sam Cooke: "You Send Me"

❁ Jackie Wilson: "(Your Love Keeps Lifting Me) Higher and Higher"

❁ Otis Redding: "(Sittin' On) The Dock of the Bay"

❁ Lou Rawls: "You'll Never Find Another Love Like Mine"

❁ Marvin Gaye: "I Heard It Through the Grapevine"

❁ Al Green: "Let's Stay Together"

❁ Gladys Knight & the Pips: "Midnight Train to Georgia"

The subsequent chapters profile nine great African-American musical artists who specialized in rock 'n' roll, soul, or both. Not only has their music brought great joy to our lives, but each has also lived an extraordinary life. These are their stories.

Chuck Berry performing in 1973

Chuck Berry

Jerry Lee Lewis, the explosive white rock 'n' roller of the 1950s, never forgot what his mother told him. "You and Elvis are pretty good," she said, "but you're no Chuck Berry."[1]

Mrs. Lewis meant no disrespect to her son or to Elvis Presley. But Berry is the "Father of Rock 'n' Roll." He did not invent the music genre; no single individual can make that claim. However, according to the Rock and Roll Hall of Fame, "Chuck Berry comes the closest of any single figure to being the one who put all the essential pieces together. It was his particular genius to graft country & western guitar licks onto a rhythm & blues chassis in his very first single, 'Maybellene.'"[2]

Up until the mid–1950s, rhythm and blues was popular among African Americans. But some artists, including Berry, added a strong guitar element and emphasized the backbeat in their songs. Disc jockey Alan Freed called this new sound "rock 'n' roll." Black and white teenagers went crazy for the music, particularly when Berry performed it. He engaged his audiences by singing fun songs about things teenagers liked—such as cars and young love. "As I was motivatin' over the hill," he sings, "I saw Maybellene in a coupe de ville."

At some of the early rock 'n' roll shows, organizers ran a rope down the middle of the floor to separate black and white audience members. But rock 'n' rollers such as Berry broke down the barriers. While touring with Fats Domino in the 1950s, Berry saw audiences begin to integrate. "Salt and pepper all mixed together," Berry said, "and we'd say, 'Well, look what's happening.'"[3]

From Boyhood to "Maybellene"

On October 18, 1926, Charles Edward Anderson "Chuck" Berry was born into a middle-class family in St. Louis, Missouri. His father was a church deacon, and his mother and five siblings loved to sing hymns. "As far back as I can remember, mother's household chanting of those gospel tunes rang through my childhood," Berry remembered. "The members of the family, regardless of what they were doing at the time, had a habit of joining with another member who would start singing, following along and harmonizing. Looking back I'm sure that my musical roots were planted, then and there."[4]

As a teenager, Berry emulated such blues greats as Muddy Waters. When he performed his own blues song at a high school event, the kids went nuts. Unfortunately, as a seventeen-year-old in 1944, Berry derailed his music career. He and two other adolescents went on a robbery spree. Although Berry carried a gun that he knew was broken, he was convicted of armed robbery and sentenced to reform school. He was not released until his twenty-first birthday.

Afterward, Berry decided to make something of his life. He worked at a General Motors plant, and at night he studied hairdressing and cosmetology. He also developed his guitar skills, and in 1952 he formed a trio with a pianist and a drummer. They played everything from blues and ballads to calypso and country. Later, Berry entertained African Americans at the Cosmopolitan Club in St. Louis. He added some country-and-western riffs (short, repeated musical phrases) to create a hillbilly sound, which attracted white patrons to the club.

Berry's big break came in 1955. After watching his idol, Muddy Waters, play in a Chicago blues club, he asked Waters how he could get a record made. Waters told him to go to Chess Records on Chicago's South Side. Leonard Chess asked Berry to produce a demo tape, and a few days later Berry returned with one in hand. Mr. Chess liked Berry's hillbilly song "Ida May," which would be renamed "Maybellene." Chess signed Berry to a record contract, and that summer "Maybellene" caught the nation's attention. It soared to No. 1 on the R&B (rhythm and blues) chart and No. 5 on the pop chart. Chuck Berry had become an overnight sensation.

Rhythm Supreme

In the mid-to-late 1950s, rock 'n' roll exploded onto the scene. Stars such as Elvis Presley, Jerry Lee Lewis, Little Richard, and Buddy Holly rocked the airwaves and performed in movies and on television. With his electric guitar, bopping beat, and showmanship, Berry epitomized rock 'n' roll. He engaged audiences with his smile and facial expressions, and he created a "duck walk" dance with his guitar that drove fans wild. As a rock 'n' roll lyricist, Berry was unmatched. "I got the rockin' pneumonia, I need a shot of rhythm and blues," he sings in his 1956 hit "Roll Over Beethoven." "Roll over Beethoven and tell Tchaikovsky the news."

15

Chuck Berry doing his famous "duck walk" onstage in 1965

From 1957 to 1959, Berry placed more than a dozen songs on the pop charts. Some would become all-time classics, including "Rock and Roll Music," "Sweet Little Sixteen," and "Johnny B. Goode." Decades later, *Rolling Stone* ranked "Johnny B. Goode" as the seventh greatest rock song of all time. The song even inspired a movie, *Go, Johnny, Go!* (1959), in which Berry appeared.

In December 1959, at the peak of his success, Berry again ran afoul of the law. He was arrested for bringing a fourteen-year-old girl from Mexico to work in his club in St. Louis. (It was a felony to transport a woman across state lines "for immoral purposes.") Found guilty, he was incarcerated from 1962 to 1964.

By the time of his release, a new generation of rockers was emerging. Many of them had been influenced by Berry. In 1963, the Beach Boys released "Surfin' USA," which paired Berry's melody for "Sweet Little Sixteen" with new lyrics. The Beatles also learned from the "master." "If you tried to give rock and roll another name," John Lennon declared, "you might call it 'Chuck Berry.'"[5]

Keith Richards, the legendary guitarist of the Rolling Stones, admired Berry's craftsmanship. "To me, Chuck Berry always was the epitome of rhythm and blues playing, rock and roll playing," Richards said. "It was beautiful, effortless, and his timing was perfection. He is rhythm supreme."[6]

Though the style of rock music changed dramatically in the mid-1960s, Berry still found some success. "No Particular Place to Go" (No. 10 on the pop chart) was one of his five top-100 releases in 1964–1965. Afterward, his career declined. Except for the 1972 novelty song "My Ding-a-Ling," which ironically was the only No. 1 song of his career, Berry's days as a hitmaker were over.

17

Career Highlights

✻ Charles Edward Anderson Berry

✻ "Father of Rock 'n' Roll"

✻ Born: October 18, 1926

✻ Hometown: St. Louis, Missouri

✻ Genre: rock 'n' roll

✻ Skills: singer, songwriter, guitarist

✻ First record: 1955

✻ Placed fifteen songs on the R&B Top Ten chart

✻ Ranked No. 5 on *Rolling Stone*'s list of "The Immortals" of rock music

✻ Inspired such legendary artists as Elvis Presley, the Beatles, and the Rolling Stones

✻ Known for his "duck walk"

His legacy, however, lived on. In 1979, at the request of President Jimmy Carter, Berry performed at the White House. Three years later, Chess Records released *The Great Twenty-Eight*—a collection of Berry's greatest hits from 1955 to 1965. *Rolling Stone* rated it the twenty-first greatest album of all time. Berry received the Grammy Lifetime Achievement Award in 1984, and in 1986 he was among the first class of inductees into the Rock and Roll Hall of Fame.

Berry performed at President Bill Clinton's 1993 inaugural, and he continued to tour into the 21st century. In fact, in 2008, he embarked on a worldwide tour. His schedule included shows in a dozen countries, from Brazil to Russia—all this at the age of eighty-one!

In 2004, *Rolling Stone* again honored Berry, ranking him No. 5 on its list of rock immortals. Only the Beatles, Bob Dylan, Elvis Presley, and the Rolling Stones (in that order) were ranked ahead of him. But other critics, such as Jerry Lee Lewis's mother and the great Stevie Wonder, might put Berry even higher on the list. "There's only one true king of rock 'n' roll," Wonder said. "His name is Chuck Berry."[7]

Chuck Berry Timeline

May 21, 1955—Records "Maybellene," his first hit record.

June 30, 1956—"Roll Over Beethoven" reaches No. 2 on the R&B chart.

September–November 1957—Tours with the "Biggest Show of Stars for '57."

March 17, 1958—"Sweet Little Sixteen" reaches No. 2 on pop chart, while "Johnny B. Goode" sits at No. 8.

May 31, 1961—Opens an amusement park, called Berryland, outside St. Louis.

October 21, 1972—"My Ding-a-Ling" becomes his first, and only, No. 1 record.

June 1, 1979—Performs for President Jimmy Carter.

February 26, 1985—Receives a Lifetime Achievement Award at the Grammys.
January 23, 1986—Is inducted into the Rock and Roll Hall of Fame.

1987—Is honored in the film *Hail! Hail! Rock and Roll*.

2004—Is ranked #5 on *Rolling Stone*'s list of "rock immortals".

2011—Performes at a New Year's Day concert in Chicago.

Ray Charles

Ray Charles Robinson was a student at the Florida School for the Deaf and Blind in 1945 when he got called into the principal's office. He was told that he needed to pack his bags and go home right away. Something serious had happened.

Arriving in his hometown of Greenville, Florida—a rural, segregated community—the blind teenager heard the news: His mother, Aretha Robinson, just thirty-two years old, had died from food poisoning.

Ray was in a state of shock. His mother had meant the world to him, and now he'd never be with her again. Just fourteen years old, he didn't know how to cope. For days, he couldn't eat. He couldn't sleep. He didn't cry or express his feelings. Family friends tried to console him, but they couldn't get through. "I was truly a lost child," Charles said.[1]

Finally, a kind, elderly woman named Ma Beck talked to the grieving teen. She knew all about Ray's upbringing—how his father had been gone most of the time, working for the railroad. And how Ray, as a five-year-old child, had tried to rescue his younger brother,

21

Ray Charles in
France in 1967

who had drowned in a large tub of water. Ma Beck knew that Ray had gradually lost his eyesight (due to glaucoma), beginning at age five. She knew that his mother had taught Ray to be independent, to be ready for the day when his sight would fail altogether. She knew about the heartbreaking day when his mother sent her seven-year-old boy on a train to a specialized school that was 160 miles away. She understood the hardships.

"Son," Ma Beck said, "you know that I knew your mama. And I know how she tried to raise you. And I know she always taught you to carry on."[2] With words of compassion, Ma Beck continued to talk to Ray about the loss of his mother…and his brother. And as she talked, Ray began to cry. The tears, bottled up for so many days, poured like rain.

"That episode with Ma Beck shook me out of my depression," Charles said. "It really started me on my way. After that I told myself that I must do what my mom would have expected me to do. And so the two greatest tragedies in my life—losing my brother and then my mom—were, strangely enough, extraordinarily positive for me. What I've accomplished since then, really, grows out of my coming to terms with those events."[3]

From his mother, Ray learned how to be independent. Despite his disability, he refused to rely on canes or seeing-eye dogs. He instead tried to find his way on his own. He learned to use a typewriter and to play an array of musical instruments. Ray also learned to sing from his heart…and his soul.

He could sing gospel, jazz, country, and blues, but he made his mark as the "father of soul music." Love, pain, pathos, and joy—all the feelings that churned within him—came bursting forth in his soulful ballads. His versions of "Georgia on My Mind," "Somewhere Over the

23

Jamie Foxx as Ray Charles in the 2004 movie *Ray*. Foxx won an Academy Award for his portrayal of Ray Charles.

Rainbow," and "America the Beautiful" have mesmerized and inspired audiences worldwide.

"That grin, that voice, his music is so joyous," said fellow music legend Elton John. "Anything he put out, I bought. He has one of the greatest voices of all time."[4]

Ray's Way

Born on September 23, 1930, in Albany, Georgia, Ray fell in love with music at an early age. As a toddler, he liked to bang on the piano at the Red Wing Café in Greenville, Florida. A patient musician named Wylie Pitman showed him how to play piano the right way. Ray loved all kinds of music. He sang in the Shiloh Baptist Church choir, and he enjoyed the blues and boogie-woogie that he heard on the café's jukebox.

Though just an average student, Ray proved extraordinary in the music room at the St. Augustine (Florida) School for the Deaf and Blind. He learned to play piano as well as the trumpet, alto sax, clarinet, and organ. Though his teachers taught only classical music, Ray liked to experiment with jazz and blues. He loved to emulate his idol, Nat King Cole, a piano player and honey-smooth jazz singer. As a young teenager, Ray learned to create musical arrangements. He enjoyed the thrill of creating his very own music.

Not long after his mother died, Ray tried to make it as a musician. He scraped out a living playing gigs in Florida, most notably as a piano player and part-time singer with a white country-and-western band. When the band traveled, Ray was forced to use "blacks only" facilities such as restrooms. Also during this time, he started taking heroin—a highly addictive and life-threatening drug. He would battle this addiction well into the 1960s.

In 1948, Ray tired of Florida. He saved about $500 and moved to Seattle. Ray thrived in his new city, where he formed a small jazz and blues band called the Maxim Trio. Not wanting to be confused with boxing superstar Sugar Ray Robinson, he changed his name to Ray Charles. In 1949, Swingtime Records offered him a big break—a chance to make his own records. Beginning with "Confession Blues," he released several records with the label. In 1951, he entered the R&B charts for the first time with "Baby Let Me Hold Your Hand." A year later, the prominent record company Atlantic Records purchased his contract from Swingtime. He was headed for stardom.

With Atlantic, Charles shed his habit of imitating Nat King Cole. He developed his own soulful style. "I'd been singing spirituals since I was three and I'd been singing the blues for just as long," Charles said. "So what could be more natural than to combine them?… All the sounds were there, right at the top of my head."[5]

A Genius and Legend

In 1954, Charles climbed to No. 7 on the R&B chart with "It Should Have Been Me." He recorded his debut album, *Ray Charles*, in 1957, and brought down the house with his performance at the 1958 Newport Jazz Festival. With his new background singers, the Raelettes, Charles soared to No. 1 on the R&B charts with the lively "What'd I Say" in 1959. Decades later, *Rolling Stone* would rank it as the tenth-greatest song of all time.

By November 1960, when his single "Georgia on My Mind" hit No. 1 on the pop charts, all of America knew about Ray Charles. He stole the show at the 1961 Grammy Awards. He won two Grammys for "Georgia on My Mind" and one each for the album *The Genius of Ray Charles* and the song "Let the Good Times Roll."

Career Highlights

❈ Ray Charles Robinson

❈ "Genius"

❈ Born: September 23, 1930

❈ Died: June 10, 2004

❈ Hometown: Albany, Georgia

❈ Genres: R&B, soul, blues, gospel, pop, jazz, country

❈ Skills: singer, songwriter, pianist, arranger

❈ First record: 1949

❈ Won the Kennedy Center Lifetime Achievement Award

❈ Received the Grammy Lifetime Achievement Award

❈ Ranked No. 10 on *Rolling Stone*'s list of greatest musical artists

❈ His version of "Georgia on My Mind" is the state song of Georgia.

That fall, "Hit the Road Jack"—his most famous original recording—zoomed to No. 1 on the pop charts.

Charles proved adept at soul, jazz, R&B, big band, and country and western. He won Grammys for best R&B recordings in 1963 ("I Can't Stop Loving You") and 1964 ("Busted"). Everyone, it seemed, loved the energy, humanity, and unique sounds of Charles's music. For the rest of the century and beyond, he toured the world and made celebrated appearances on network television.

All kinds of honors followed. His 1978 autobiography, *Brother Ray*, became a bestseller. In 1979, "Georgia on My Mind" was adopted as the official song of the state of Georgia. Two years later, Charles received a star on Hollywood Boulevard's Walk of Fame. He was among the first musicians inducted into the Rock and Roll Hall of Fame, in 1986. And in 1993, he performed at the inauguration of one of his biggest fans, President Bill Clinton. Later in the year, the president presented him with the National Medal of Arts.

Ray Charles lived an unconventional life. Married twice, he fathered twelve children with nine different women. He was generous toward charities and his children. Before dying from liver cancer in 2004, he willed $1 million to each of his children, plus $1 million to Dillard University and $2 million each to Morehouse College and Albany State University.

That same year, the film and music industry made sure that his legend lived on. Five months after his death, the movie *Ray*—starring Jamie Foxx in an Oscar-winning performance—appeared in theaters. Also, Charles's final album, *Genius Loves Company*, was released. The album included duets in which Charles teamed with such greats as Johnny Mathis, B. B. King, Van Morrison, and Willie Nelson. The album won eight Grammy Awards.

Johnny Mathis had sold more than 350 million records, but performing with the "the Genius" was something special. "I was so nervous to be in the same studio as Ray Charles," Mathis said. "He is not just an ordinary singer, musician, or icon. He's the best of the best."[6]

Ray Charles Timeline

1949—Changes his name to Ray Charles and releases his first single, "Confession Blues."

1954—Releases his first hit record, "It Should Have Been Me."

July 1958—Makes a splash with his performance at the Newport Jazz Festival.

1959—Releases the album *The Genius of Ray Charles*.

August 1959—Releases the revolutionary song "What'd I Say," which will soar to No. 1 on the R&B chart.

November 1960—"Georgia on My Mind" reaches No. 1 on the pop chart.

April 12, 1961—Wins four Grammy Awards, including two for "Georgia on My Mind."

October 1961—"Hit the Road Jack" lands at No. 1 on the pop chart.

January 1985—Contributes to the song "We Are the World," the proceeds of which go to hunger relief in Africa.

January 23, 1986—Among the first group of inductees for the Rock and Roll Hall of Fame.

February 13, 2005—*Genius Loves Company* wins eight Grammy Awards.

Little Richard at his piano in 1957

Chapter 3

Little Richard

With one outlandish word, "A-wop-bop-a-loo-mop-a-whop-bam-boom!", Little Richard lit the fuse that ignited rock 'n' roll.

It all started in September 1955. Little Richard, age twenty-two, had been performing and making records—which weren't very successful—since 1951. When he got a chance to record for Specialty Records in New Orleans in 1955, Specialty producer Robert "Bumps" Blackwell was not impressed. First of all, Blackwell could not believe the outrageousness of Little Richard, whose hair, Blackwell claimed, was a foot high. His shirt, Blackwell said, "was so loud it looked as though he had drunk raspberry juice, cherryade, malt, and greens, and then thrown up all over himself."[1] Little Richard chose to record slow blues songs for Specialty that were not especially good.

During a break that day, Blackwell and Richard went to the Dew Drop Inn. Noticing an unused piano, Richard began to play. The flamboyant musician let loose. He jackhammered the keys while blaring the words of a risqué boogie-woogie song called "Tutti Frutti." His shrieking, raspy voice—punctuated with high-pitched

31

"woooos"—captivated Blackwell. After local lyricist Dorothy LaBostrie altered the lyrics, Blackwell and Richard returned to the studio to record "Tutti Frutti."

This was Little Richard's big chance, and he was determined to make the most of it. He opened with "A-wop-bop-a-loo-mop-a-whop-bam-boom," and he didn't let up. "I was singing at the top of my voice," he recalled. "I was screaming…you never seen a guy with a big head like me scream as loud as I was hollering. I made up this song and I screamed, and played, and banged on the piano; I think I almost tore that piano out of the wall…I brought the rock 'n' roll in there."[2]

At the time in 1955, rock 'n' roll was in its infancy. "Rock Around the Clock" by Bill Haley and His Comets—the first popular rock 'n' roll record—became a hit that spring. Elvis Presley was not yet a major star, and Chuck Berry's music first hit the airwaves that summer. Then came Little Richard, whose new hit record shocked Americans from coast to coast. Conservatives—and there were plenty of them in 1955—were appalled by the sound and attitude of "Tutti Frutti." But teenagers shook, rattled, and rolled to the funky new beat. They wanted more and more of Little Richard, and the artist and Specialty Records happily obliged.

Between September 1955 and October 1957, Little Richard recorded fifty songs. From this material, Specialty released nine singles and two albums. "Long Tall Sally" and other songs soared up the charts, and his live performances blew the roof off the dance halls. He appeared on television and, in 1956, in two rock 'n' roll movies: *Don't Knock the Rock* and *The Girl Can't Help It*. Richard wore sequined vests, a pompadour hairstyle, and heavy makeup, and he sang with a wild look in his eyes. When he threw his leg on the piano while

Little Richard

Little Richard performed during the halftime show at the AutoZone Liberty Bowl in Memphis, Tennessee, December 31, 2004.

still pounding on the keys, the audience went wild. Never before, and never again, would there be another Little Richard.

Yelling and Screaming

The legacy of Little Richard began on December 5, 1932. Richard Wayne Penniman entered the world with all the odds stacked against him. He was born during the Great Depression in the heart of the segregated South. One of twelve children, he grew up in an impoverished area of a poor city: Macon, Georgia. Music, however, enriched his life. Throughout his neighborhood, evangelists and vendors sang to capture people's attention. Moreover, Richard's father was a preacher, and his family loved to sing gospel hymns. In fact, they formed a group called the Penniman Singers. They sang in churches and entered singing contests.

A high-energy child, Richard also loved to sing—if you could call it that. "I thought he couldn't sing . . . just a noise," said one of his brothers, "and he would get on your nerves hollerin' and beating on tin cans and things of that nature. People around would get angry and upset with him yelling and screaming."[3]

But young Richard was destined to perform, and as a young teenager he left home to join Sugarfoot Sam's Minstrel Show. By winning a talent show in 1951, he landed a contract with RCA Victor. Though his four records fell flat, he continued to plug away. In Macon, he washed dishes at a bus station's cafeteria during the day and played the blues at the Tick Tock Club at night. A musician named Esquerita showed him some flamboyant techniques on the piano. Meanwhile, Richard copied the look of blues musician Bill Wright, who wore eyeliner, "tall hair," and splashy outfits.

After his RCA disappointments, Little Richard recorded songs for Peacock Records. His early 1955 tune "Little Richard's Boogie" offered a glimpse of what was to come. His "Tutti Frutti" was so big that other singers tried to ride it to success. Elvis twice sang it on national television, and white singer Pat Boone's mild version rose to No. 12 on the pop chart. In 1956 and 1957, Little Richard charted with "Long Tall Sally," Slippin' and Slidin'," "Rip It Up," "Lucille," "Send Me Some Lovin'," "Jenny, Jenny," and "Keep a Knockin'." Then the music stopped.

Mixing God and Rock

At the time, Little Richard and some other Americans felt there was something immoral and un-Christian about this new kind of music. "If you want to live with the Lord, you can't rock 'n' roll it, too," Richard would later say. "God doesn't like it."[4] In October 1957, during a performance in Australia, Little Richard received what he felt was a sign from God. The Soviet Union had launched Sputnik, the first-ever satellite, which people could see orbiting around the earth.

"It looked as though the big ball of fire came directly over the stadium about two or three hundred feet above our heads," Richard said. "It shook my mind. It really shook my mind. I got up from the piano and said, 'This is it. I am through. I am leaving show business to go back to God!'"[5]

And he did. In January 1958, he started classes at Oakwood Theological College in Alabama. While his big hit "Good Golly, Miss Molly" ruled the airwaves that spring, he was studying to become a Seventh Day Adventist preacher. Little Richard returned to music in 1959, but this time as a gospel singer. When he drifted back to rock 'n' roll in 1962, promoters opened their arms to him.

35

Career Highlights

❋ Richard Wayne Penniman

❋ Born: December 5, 1932

❋ Hometown: Macon, Georgia

❋ Genres: rock 'n' roll, gospel, R&B

❋ Skills: singer, songwriter, pianist, keyboardist

❋ First record: 1951

❋ Sold 32 million records by 1968

❋ Ranked No. 8 on *Rolling Stone*'s list of all-time greatest rock artists

❋ Fourth winner of the Rhythm & Blues Foundation's Pioneer Lifetime Achievement Award

❋ His "Tutti Frutti" topped *Mojo*'s list of the songs that "changed the world."

He shared a bill with the Beatles in Germany, and the Rolling Stones opened for him during a 1963 European tour. A young Jimi Hendrix played in Little Richard's band for several months in 1965. Hendrix would say a year later, "I want to do with my guitar what Little Richard does with his voice."[6]

Little Richard would record more rock and gospel music, but without much commercial success. In the 1970s, after battling drug and alcohol abuse, he again returned to the ministry. In the mid–1980s, he was in the news again. The 1984 biography *The Life and Times of Little Richard* captivated readers, and in 1985 he survived a serious auto accident. In 1986, he appeared in the hit movie *Down and Out in Beverly Hills*, which included his hit song "Great Gosh a 'Mighty." That same year, he was among the original class of inductees enshrined in the Rock and Roll Hall of Fame.

In the late 1980s, Little Richard fused his two passions together. During performances, he played both gospel music and his old hits. He preached the word of God onstage and distributed Christian literature. Little Richard remained active for the next two decades. In 1993, he performed for President Bill Clinton's inauguration.

In 2004, *Rolling Stone* ranked Little Richard at No. 8 on its list of the 100 greatest rock artists of all time. Most of those who ranked ahead of him had claimed that Richard had influenced them. They included the Beatles, Elvis, Bob Dylan, and the Rolling Stones.

In June 2007, *Mojo: The Music Magazine* published "Big Bangs: 100 Records That Changed the World." Elvis ranked third with "Heartbreak Hotel," and the Beatles placed second with "I Want to Hold Your Hand." And the one record that most changed the world? Little Richard's "Tutti Frutti." "One can only imagine," the magazine editors pondered, "how it must have sounded when the song exploded across the airwaves!"[7]

It sounded like this: "A-wop-bop-a-loo-mop-a-whop-bam-boom!"

Little Richard Timeline

September 1955—Records "Tutti Frutti," which will become his first hit.

1956—Performs three songs in the film *The Girl Can't Help It*.

April 1, 1956—"Long Tall Sally," his biggest hit, tops the R&B chart for the first of eight weeks.

June 30, 1956—"Slippin' and Slidin'" rises to No. 2 on the R&B chart.

August 4, 1956—"Rip It Up" goes to No. 1 on the R&B chart.

April 13, 1957—"Lucille" hits No. 1 on the R&B chart.

January 1958—Enters Oakwood Theological College in Huntsville, Alabama.

May 17, 1958—"Good Golly, Miss Molly" hits No. 4 on the R&B chart.

1959—Releases the album *Little Richard Sings Gospel*.

Fall 1962—Makes a rock 'n' roll comeback, sharing a bill with the Beatles.

January 23, 1986—Inducted into the Rock and Roll Hall of Fame.

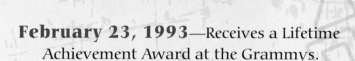

February 23, 1993—Receives a Lifetime Achievement Award at the Grammys.

1994—Receives a Lifetime Achievement Award from the Rhythm & Blues Foundation.

2002—Receives NAACP Image Award—Hall of Fame Award.

2003—Inducted into the Songwriters Hall of Fame.

2007—"Tutti Frutti" tops *Mojo* magazine's list of "100 Records That Changed the World"; in 2010 the recording is added to the Library of Congress's National Recording Registry.

James Brown
in the 1950s

Chapter 4

James Brown

On Tuesday night, James Brown was having a heart attack. Then he had another on Wednesday, Thursday, Friday, and Saturday! At least, that's the way it seemed.

The "Hardest Working Man in Show Business," Brown sometimes performed more than three hundred shows a year. He was a human dynamo—singing, screaming, dancing, sweating…almost convulsing. He became possessed by the music. At the climax of each show, while screaming himself hoarse, he fell to his knees. Anguished, he cradled the microphone stand as if holding a dying loved one in his arms. The crowd wailed. On cue, a member of the band—looking gravely concerned—approached the fallen star. Then another brought a long cape and draped it over the "stricken" singer's shoulders.

With the band still playing, and with Brown seemingly on the verge of collapse, the men began to escort him from the stage. But then he stopped, shook his shoulders violently, and whipped off the cape. Willing himself back to life, he stutter-stepped to the microphone and wailed through the rest of the performance. The crowd went wild. Every night.

Back from the Dead

Everything about James Brown seemed cloaked in high drama—even his birth. "I was stillborn," he said about the eventful day on May 3, 1933, in Barnwell, South Carolina. "The midwives laid me aside, thought I was really gone. I laid there about an hour, and they picked me back up and tried again, 'cause my body was still warm. The Good Lord brought me back."[1]

Had Brown not survived, popular music as we know it could have been remarkably different. Brown took traditional R&B to a higher level. Moreover, he was called the "Godfather of Soul"—in other words, that genre's originator. He also pioneered funk music, and is considered a forefather of rap. Amazingly, 114 of his songs hit *Billboard* magazine's R&B singles charts, and 94 of them cracked the pop charts. The Rock and Roll Hall of Fame declared, "What Elvis Presley was to rock and roll, James Brown became to R&B: a prolific and dominant phenom [phenomenon]."[2]

After his traumatic entry into the world, Brown endured a troubled childhood. The product of a broken home, he lived with relatives and friends in a poor area of Augusta, Georgia. As a youth, he picked cotton, shined shoes, and danced in public for coins. After being arrested at age sixteen for breaking into cars, he was sent to reform school.

That experience turned his life around. While incarcerated, Brown met singer Bobby Byrd, the leader of a gospel music group. After his release, Brown joined Byrd's group. They sang gospel for a while, but couldn't resist the urge to play rhythm and blues. They changed the name of their group to the Flames and toured the South's "chitlin circuit" of clubs that welcomed African-American performers. Though their music

James Brown performs during a Java Jazz Festival concert in Jakarta, Indonesia, in 2005.

was labeled R&B, the band infused the fervor of gospel into their performances.

As a songwriter, singer, and dancer, Brown was the star of the show. By 1956, he and the Flames had their first big hit, "Please, Please, Please," which sold more than a million copies. Brown built his fan base by booking shows nearly every night. Moreover, he poured his all into every performance. He danced all night and often did the splits (despite wearing his famous skintight pants). Allegedly, he sweated off seven pounds a night. "My expectations of other people, I double them on myself," he said.[3]

In 1958, Brown's "Try Me" rocketed to No. 1 on the R&B chart—the first of seventeen of his songs to do so. Despite his popularity among African Americans, he did not cross over to white audiences until 1963. That year, his *Live at the Apollo* album became a national hit. "There is no fat here," music critic Will Fulford-Jones wrote about the album. "Brown and musical director Lewis Hamlin had drilled their band to an immaculate, fiery precision; there is barely room for the eight-strong horn section to catch its collective breath."[4]

King of Funk

In 1965, Brown introduced funk to the music scene with "Papa's Got a Brand New Bag." Funk was not about melody and harmony. Instead, it emphasized a steady rhythm with drumlike vocals and punchy horns. Like a quick-fisted boxer, Brown and his band peppered listeners with rapid-fire musical blows. "Papa's Got a Brand New Bag" and 1965's "I Got You (I Feel Good)" became Brown's first Top Ten hits on the pop charts.

Around that time, Brown starred in the concert film *The T.A.M.I. Show*. Numerous acts appeared in the movie,

but Brown outshone them all. "You have the Rolling Stones on the same stage, all of the important rock acts of the day, doing their best—and James Brown comes out and destroys them," wrote producer Rick Rubin in *Rolling Stone*.[5]

Through the rest of the 1960s and into the 1970s, Brown immersed himself in funk. "I was hearing everything, even the guitars, like they were drums," he said.[6] Yet simultaneously, he was hailed as the Godfather of Soul.

In the late 1960s, Brown became a "spokes-singer" for the civil rights movement. His 1966 song "Don't Be a Drop-Out" urged black children to stay in school. In 1968, in "Operation Black Pride," he dressed as Santa Claus. He handed out certificates for free Christmas dinners to poor Africans Americans in New York City. In 1968, he recorded a song that said it all: "Say It Loud— I'm Black and I'm Proud." The song became an anthem for the country's black pride movement.

Brown weathered troubled times in the 1970s. In 1973, he lost his first son, Teddy, in an auto accident. He suffered through financial, legal, and family problems. With the emergence of disco music, Americans lost interest in Brown's style. His attempt at the new genre, the album *The Original Disco Man*, flopped.

The 1980s were another period of highs and lows. Brown's performance as a singing preacher in *The Blues Brothers* brought moviegoers to their feet. When rap music emerged later in the decade, Brown gained a newfound respect. Rappers reached into his collection of eight hundred songs and found grooves that worked for them. Brown's 1985 single "Living in America" was a hit, and in 1986 he was among the first group of inductees to the Rock and Roll Hall of Fame. But he also spent three

45

years in prison, beginning on December 15, 1988, for failing to stop for a police officer and aggravated assault.

As the new century dawned, Brown returned to social activism. Troubled by the rise in school shootings, he wrote a song called "Killing's Out and School's In." "We need to protect the kids by giving them something to do,"

Career Highlights

❋ James Joseph Brown, Jr.

❋ "Godfather of Soul"

❋ Born: May 3, 1933

❋ Hometown: Barnwell, South Carolina

❋ Died: December 25, 2006

❋ Genres: R&B, soul, funk, gospel

❋ Skills: singer, songwriter, bandleader, multi-instrumentalist, dancer, record producer

❋ First record: 1956

❋ Credited with more than eight hundred songs

❋ Placed ninety-four songs on the Hot 100 singles charts

❋ Performed more than three hundred shows in a year at the peak of his career

❋ Received the Grammy Lifetime Achievement Award

he said. "[It's about] making them interested, making them love mom and dad more, love the family more, love themselves more, and love their school. So there won't have to be killing in school."[7]

Brown continued performing, but by 2006 his body had worn down. The man who had entered the world so dramatically also left it in dramatic fashion. On Christmas Day in 2006, he lay dying of heart failure in an Atlanta hospital. He announced to Charles Bobbit, his personal manager, "I'm going away tonight."[8] He then took three final breaths and closed his eyes. The hardest working man in show business would finally rest in peace.

James Brown Timeline

April 11, 1956—"Please, Please, Please" by James Brown and the Famous Flames hits No. 6 on the R&B chart.

1958—"Try Me" is the best-selling R&B single of the year.

June 30, 1963—*Live at the Apollo* is released. It will soar to No. 2 on the album chart.

1964—Steals the show in the concert film *The T.A.M.I. Show*.

February 1, 1965—Records the revolutionary funk song "Papa's Got a Brand New Bag."

1968—Makes a statement with the song "Say It Loud—I'm Black and I'm Proud."

1980—Delivers a memorable performance as a preacher in the film *The Blues Brothers*.

January 11, 1986—Hits No. 4 on the pop chart with "Living in America."

January 23, 1986—Among the first group to be inducted into the Rock and Roll Hall of Fame.

December 1, 2003—Receives a Kennedy Center Honor.

Chapter 5

Aretha Franklin

Floating in cyberspace is a video of Aretha Franklin performing on an early 1960s TV show called *Shindig*. Fans may not recognize her. Dressed conservatively, with a white woman's hairdo, Franklin smiles and plays the piano. She sings "Rock-A-Bye Your Baby with a Dixie Melody." The pleasing, mild song had been popularized in the 1920s by Al Jolson, a white singer who performed in blackface. Franklin finishes the song and bows to the nearly all-white audience. A nice performance, but she could have done better. She just needed the opportunity to express herself.

For five years, Franklin had played the mild music that Columbia Records insisted she play. Columbia, said record producer John Hammond, "misunderstood her genius."[1] But in 1966, Franklin signed with Atlantic Records, which specialized in rhythm and blues. Backed by a funky rhythm section, she got the chance to let it all hang out.

Her first album with Atlantic, *I Never Loved a Man the Way I Loved You*, was a runaway smash. Franklin unleashed the full power of her four-octave voice. Jon

Aretha Franklin in a recording studio around 1961

Pareles of the *New York Times* recalled that "her voice leaped heavenward as she used the fervor of gospel singing to capture the joys and pains of secular love."[2] The title track from that album sold a million copies in 1967. The album flew off the shelves, as fans couldn't get enough of the new singing sensation. "Aretha's music," said soul musician Bobby Taylor, "makes you sweaty, gives you a chill, makes you want to stomp your feet."[3]

"Respect", the album's biggest hit, served as the unofficial anthem for the burgeoning women's rights movement. "All I'm askin'," she sings to her man, "is for a little respect when you come home." And if she didn't make that clear, she spells it out for him: "R–E–S–P–E–C–T." Women loved it, and men got the message.

A Preacher's Daughter

Born in Memphis, Tennessee, on March 25, 1942, Franklin inherited her booming voice from her parents. Her mother, Barbara Siggers Franklin, was a supremely talented singer. Her father, Reverend C. L. Franklin, inspired thousands with his fiery sermons. Aretha and her four siblings grew up in Detroit, where Reverend Franklin was the pastor of the New Bethel Baptist Church. Reverend Franklin's preaching aroused such passions that two nurses stood by to aid parishioners.

When Aretha was six, her parents separated, with her mother moving to Buffalo, New York. The children lived with their father during the school year and spent the summers with their mother. Reverend Franklin earned a comfortable living as a minister. The Franklins lived in a large house in Detroit—although on the fringes of a low-income neighborhood. The reverend knew hundreds of people, and musicians and singers were among the many visitors. Musicians such as Mahalia Jackson

and James Cleveland often came by to sing and play. Aretha soaked it all up.

In 1952, the Franklins' world was shattered when Barbara died of a heart attack. The ordeal profoundly affected Aretha and her siblings. "After her mama died," said Mahalia Jackson, "the whole family wanted for love."[4] Aretha found solace by singing gospel music in her father's church. She performed her first solo at age twelve, drawing raves from the parishioners. Two years later, she and her father made a record. *The Gospel Soul of Aretha Franklin* included the reverend's sermons and Aretha's gospel songs.

The father and daughter took their gospel show on the road. But Aretha found touring difficult, especially during an era of segregation. Sometimes they had to drive farther and farther down the road to find a restaurant that would serve African Americans. Though unmarried, Aretha twice became pregnant as a teenager. By age seventeen, she was the mother of two boys.

At age eighteen, Aretha attracted the attention of producers at Columbia Records. For five years, she recorded what they brought her—standards, jazz tunes, and novelty songs, few of which interested her. (Aretha also felt uncomfortable touring. Shy by nature, she often sang to the floor while performing in jazz and R&B clubs.) But talent agents at Atlantic Records sensed the power and range of her voice, and saw it as a perfect fit for their R&B songs.

52

Queen of Soul

Franklin flourished after signing with Atlantic in 1966. "Respect" ranked No. 1 on *Billboard*'s R&B singles chart for a record eight weeks. In 1968, Franklin won two Grammy Awards, including one for best female R&B vocal

Aretha Franklin performing in Chicago in 2011

performance. She would go on to win that award eight years in a row! Music fans began calling it the "Aretha Award."

Franklin had a number of hits over the next few years. In "Think," her vocal range runs the gamut. "I Say a Little Prayer," a Dionne Warwick cover, is one of her signature songs. She begins the song in a soft voice and then soars to great heights. Her 1972 album *Amazing Grace* sold more than two million copies.

Ahmet Ertegun, cofounder of Atlantic Records, said of Aretha:

> I don't think there's anybody I have known who possesses an instrument like hers and who has such a thorough background in gospel, the blues, and the essential black-music idiom...She is blessed with an extraordinary combination of remarkable urban sophistication and of the deep blues feeling that comes from the [Mississippi] Delta. The result is maybe the greatest singer of our time.[5]

After rising to fame, Franklin faced professional and personal challenges. She had five children altogether, but two of her marriages ended in divorce. Even at the peak of her career, in 1968, she often seemed sad and troubled. "I don't think she's happy," said Mahalia Jackson at the time. "Somebody else is making her sing the blues."[6] In the 1970s, Aretha's career declined due to the rise of disco music. And in June 1979, she experienced a horrible tragedy. Her father was critically wounded in a burglary attempt at his home. Reverend Franklin fell into a coma, in which he remained until his death in 1984. For Aretha and her family, it was a long, painful five years.

However, the "Queen of Soul" still had a whole lot of music left in her. In 1985, she struck it big with the R&B album *Who's Zoomin' Who?* and the hit song "Freeway

Career Highlights

❊ Aretha Louise Franklin

❊ "Queen of Soul"

❊ Born: March 25, 1942

❊ Hometown: Detroit, Michigan

❊ Genres: soul, gospel, blues, pop, jazz, rock

❊ Skills: singer, songwriter, pianist

❊ First record: 1956

❊ Has won twenty Grammy Awards

❊ Won eight straight Grammys for best female R&B vocal performance

❊ Amassed more than twenty No. 1 R&B singles

❊ Has more million-sellers than any other woman in recording history

of Love." In 1987, she became the first woman inducted into the Rock and Roll Hall of Fame. That same year, she scored a No. 1 hit with "I Knew You Were Waiting (for Me)," a duet with George Michael. In March 1988, she won two Grammy Awards. She would go on to win twenty Grammys, including the Living Legend Grammy and the Lifetime Achievement Grammy.

In the 1990s, more honors followed. In 1994, she became the youngest-ever recipient of the Kennedy

Center Honors, given to artists in the performing arts. Three years later, she was inducted into the NAACP's Hall of Fame. Franklin had long been a source of pride, inspiration, and empowerment to African Americans. When Martin Luther King died in 1968, she sang at his funeral.

Now seventy, Franklin spends most of her time at home in Detroit, where she is loved and respected. In fact, the Michigan legislature once declared her voice to be one of the state's natural resources. In 2007, she recorded *Jewels in the Crown: All-Star Duets With the Queen*. The album features duets of Franklin and fellow music superstars, ranging from Frank Sinatra to Whitney Houston (her goddaughter) to Christina Aguilera and Fantasia Barrino. Franklin started her own label, Aretha's Records, with a 2008 Christmas album and the 2011 release *A Woman Falling Out of Love*. She has also been working on a musical/film based on her autobiography, *From These Roots*.

Aretha Franklin Timeline

1956—*The Gospel Sound of Aretha Franklin* is released. The singer is just fourteen years old.

November 20, 1961—"Rock-A-Bye Your Baby with a Dixie Melody," her only hit with Columbia Records, is released.

March 10, 1967—*I Never Loved a Man the Way I Love You*, her break-out album, is released.

June 3, 1967—"Respect" reaches No. 1 on the pop chart.

February 29, 1968—Wins two Grammy Awards for "Respect."

June 1, 1972—*Amazing Grace*, a powerful gospel album, is released.

July 27, 1985—"Freeway of Love" tops the R&B chart for the first of five straight weeks.

January 21, 1987—Becomes the first woman inducted into the Rock and Roll Hall of Fame.

April 18, 1987—Hits No. 1 on the pop chart with "I Knew You Were Waiting (for Me)" (with George Michael).

December 4, 1994—Becomes the youngest recipient of the Kennedy Center Honors (at age fifty-two)

March 1, 1995—Bestowed with the Grammy Lifetime Achievement Award.

September 1999—Receives the National Medal of Arts from President Bill Clinton.

November 2005—Receives Presidential Medal of Freedom from President George W. Bush.

February 2008—Receives the Vanguard Award from the National Association for the Advancement of Colored People (NAACP).

November 2008—Ranked the number one singer of the rock and roll era by *Rolling Stone* magazine.

May 2011—Releases her thirty-eighth studio album, *A Woman Falling Out of Love*, exclusively through Wal-Mart.

Chapter 6

Jimi Hendrix

It was the Summer of Love, and thousands of hippies flocked to the Monterey County Fairgrounds in California. They came to groove to some of the greatest rock and soul artists in the world—from Lou Rawls and the Who to Janis Joplin and the Grateful Dead. But during this historic Monterey Pop Festival of June 16–18, 1967, one little-known artist stole the show: Jimi Hendrix.

It was hard to describe the music he played, because no had ever heard anything like it. Some musicians called it electric blues, but to the kids in the crowd the man just rocked. Dressed in orange pants and a ruffled yellow shirt, Hendrix was the epitome of cool. A bandana held back his Afro, and he chewed gum and sang at the same time. What he did with his guitar hypnotized the crowd.

Hendrix milked every kind of sound imaginable from his decorated Fender Stratocaster, from piercing screams to harsh explosions. He played it on his knees, above his head, even behind his back. He did a tumbling roll onstage while continuing to play. During "Wild Thing," he cooed, "Come on and sssssssock it to me one time. You moooove

Jimi Hendrix acknowledges the crowd at Woodstock

me—look out!"[1] The song didn't end until Hendrix set his guitar on fire and smashed it repeatedly on the stage.

From then on, everyone knew about Jimi Hendrix.

Young and Restless

Born in Seattle, Washington, on November 27, 1942, Hendrix endured an unusual and troubled childhood. His mother was just seventeen years old when he was born, and his father was serving in the army. Originally named Johnny Hendrix, he was later renamed James (and Jimmy) by his father. Three of his four siblings had physical disabilities, including a sister who was blind. Their parents divorced when Jimmy was nine, and their mother died in 1958. The children lived in multiple homes and facilities.

Jimmy performed poorly in school, and in ninth grade he got an F in music class. Nevertheless, he loved listening to music. Blues greats Muddy Waters and Howlin' Wolf were among his favorites, as were rock 'n' roll sensations Elvis Presley and Little Richard. The Hendrixes were so poor that for a while, the closest thing Jimmy could find to a guitar was a one-stringed ukulele. In 1959, his father bought him an electric guitar, which he played left-handed. A guitarist named Butch Snipes showed Hendrix a few tricks, such as playing it behind his back and with his teeth.

Jimmy's first gig was in the basement of a synagogue. His play was so outrageous that he was booted out between sets. Hendrix was also expelled from high school due to poor grades and absenteeism. After committing a crime, he was given the choice of going to jail or the military. He enlisted in the U.S. Army and was assigned to the 101st Airborne Division in Kentucky. However, he performed so poorly that his commanding officers

61

requested that he be discharged. Jimmy happily said good-bye to army life.

Afterward, Hendrix and Army buddy Billy Cox formed a band in Nashville called the King Kasuals. The band broke up, but Hendrix was such a talented guitarist that he found work backing various R&B, soul, and blues artists. He toured the South with such legendary singers as Sam Cooke and Jackie Wilson. He later moved to New York and was hired by the Isley Brothers, a noted R&B/rock band. He took another step up in 1965 when he got to tour with one of his idols, Little Richard.

Hendrix, however, grew restless. "I was always kept in the background...," he recalled. "I dug listening to top 40 R&B but that doesn't mean I like to play it every night."[2] Hendrix wanted to break free. He yearned to create and perform his own music, to express himself through his guitar in exciting and innovative ways.

Audio Science Fiction

In 1966, he caught his big break. While performing in New York with his new band, Jimmy James and the Blue Flames, Hendrix impressed a musician named Chas Chandler. He became Hendrix's manager and took him to England. So that Hendrix would fit in to the new psychedelic rock scene, Chandler gave him a whole new look. He changed his name to Jimi and dressed him in colorful psychedelic clothing. Hendrix became part of a trio with bassist Noel Redding and drummer Mitch Mitchell. They were called the Jimi Hendrix Experience.

The creative force of the band, Hendrix fused funk, blues, and psychedelia into an entirely new kind of sound. The trio's first single, "Hey Joe," shook the music world upon its release in December 1966. When their first

Jimi Hendrix performing

album, *Are You Experienced*, hit stores in August 1967, critics were blown away.

"[T]he songs and sounds generated by Hendrix were original, otherworldly and virtually indescribable," raved the Rock and Roll Hall of Fame. "In essence, Hendrix channeled the music of the cosmos, anchoring it to the earthy beat of rock and roll."[3] Wrote music historian Wayne Robins: "He used feedback, echo, and wah-wah, shifted between major and minor chords, unleashed dazzling runs of notes that were at once blues-based and a kind of audio science fiction."[4]

In addition to "Hey Joe," *Are You Experienced* included such classics as "Purple Haze," "Foxy Lady," and the tender "The Wind Cries Mary." However, music fans had to listen to the whole album to get the "experience." Throughout Britain and America, rock fans blared the album on their stereos. In their bedrooms and living rooms, kids young and old played along on their "air guitars."

For many young Americans, Hendrix's music reflected the turbulent times. In 1967 and 1968, war raged in Vietnam, and young men were forced to fight in faraway jungles. Moreover, in several big cities, African Americans revolted against oppressive conditions. Two champions of peace and justice, Martin Luther King Jr. and presidential candidate Robert Kennedy, were assassinated in 1968. Hendrix explained how he fit into the equation: "Lots of young people now feel they're not getting a fair deal. So they revert to something loud, harsh, almost verging on violence. If they didn't go to a concert, they might be going to a riot."[5]

The Hendrix song "Machine Gun" was political in nature. Said his girlfriend, Monika Danneman: "Jimi told me that what he was trying to express was that at every moment there are terrible things going on all over the

Career Highlights

✤ Johnny Allen Hendrix

✤ Born: November 27, 1942

✤ Hometown: Seattle, Washington

✤ Died: September 18, 1970

✤ Genres: rock, blues

✤ Skills: guitarist, singer, songwriter, record producer

✤ First record: 1966

✤ Rated the greatest guitarist of all time by *Rolling Stone*

✤ Named *Billboard's* artist of the year for 1968

✤ His recordings have been featured on approximately a hundred albums since his death.

✤ Tens of millions of his albums have been sold.

world—war, destruction, and terror, and that he wanted to open people's eyes."[6] When Hendrix performed the song at the Filmore East in New York, he dedicated it to the soldiers fighting in Vietnam.

After *Are You Experienced*, the Jimi Hendrix Experience released two more albums: *Axis: Bold as Love* (1967) and *Electric Ladyland* (1968). Axis rose to No. 3 on the U.S. chart, while *Electric Ladyland* soared to No. 1. The double-album masterpiece includes "All Along the Watchtower,"

65

a highly charged cover of a Bob Dylan song. "I liked Jimi Hendrix's record of this," Dylan said, "and ever since he died I've been doing it that way. Strange, though, how when I sing it I always feel like it's a tribute to him in some kind of way."[7]

In August 1969, Hendrix highlighted the legendary Woodstock Festival in Bethel, New York. Hendrix and his new band, Gypsy Sun and Rainbows, played sixteen songs. But it was his instrumental version of "The Star-Spangled Banner" that became rock 'n' roll legend. His guitar screeched, howled, and growled the national anthem in a performance so cool that even the anti-Establishment hippies suddenly felt patriotic.

Dead at Twenty-Seven

In 1970, Hendrix and his new band toured and worked on a new album. But he never made it through the summer. On September 18, 1970, Hendrix died after overdosing on sleeping pills. He was just twenty-seven years old. Music fans were saddened but not entirely surprised. Many rock musicians were taking drugs at the time, and some lost their lives because of it. Just sixteen days later, fellow rock icon Janis Joplin died from a drug overdose.

"When I die," Hendrix once said, "just keep playing the records."[8] And they did. Over the years, producers have churned out albums of his previously unreleased recordings. Even in the 21st century, Hendrix fans were still purchasing several million of his albums every year. They still couldn't get enough of the man *Rolling Stone* called the greatest guitarist who ever lived.

Jimi Hendrix Timeline

July 2, 1962—Receives an honorable discharge from the army.

1965— Plays guitar for Little Richard's band.

June 1, 1966—Forms a band called Jimmy James and the Blue Flames.

September 1966—Flies with his new manager, Chas Chandler, to London, where they'll form a band called the Jimi Hendrix Experience.

December 16, 1966—Releases "Hey Joe," which will be the group's first hit.

June 18, 1967—Wows the crowd at the Monterey International Pop Festival.

December 1, 1967—Releases the album *Axis: Bold as Love*.

October 25, 1968—Releases *Electric Ladyland*, which includes the hit "All Along the Watchtower."

June 29, 1969—The Jimi Hendrix Experience breaks up at the height of their success.

August 18, 1969—Highlights the Woodstock music festival with his electrifying version of "The Star Spangled Banner."

September 18, 1970—Dies in his sleep, due to a drug overdose, at age twenty-seven.

The Supremes: (l-r) Mary Wilson, Diana Ross, Cindy Birdsong

Chapter 7

Diana Ross

Diana Ross has always wanted to sing. "I must have come out of the womb that way," she wrote in her memoir *Secrets of a Sparrow*. "I used to trail after my mother when she did her household chores, the walls of our apartment swelling with music: jazz, blues, Etta James."[1]

Smokey Robinson may have been her biggest musical influence. A singer in Ross's Detroit neighborhood, Robinson was on the verge of becoming a star in 1958. Diana was a friend of his niece, and the two girls spent hours watching Smokey and his band, the Miracles, perform in his basement. That year, Ross was elated when one of Robinson's records, "Got a Job," was played on the radio.

"I knew that if he could do it, I could do it, too," she wrote. "It made me feel like nothing was impossible. At the time, I had no far-reaching dreams to become a celebrity or a movie star. I just wanted to make a record. I wanted to sing."[2]

In 1958, fourteen-year-old Diana moved with her family to Detroit's Brewster housing projects. She befriended two other girls who loved to sing: Florence Ballard and Mary Wilson. They got together and rehearsed as often as they could, "with no idea how to get to the next step," Ross wrote.[3] Little did they realize what lay ahead. The trio would evolve into the Primettes and later the Supremes (with Cindy Birdsong replacing Ballard in 1967). They became the second most popular musical group of the 1960s, trailing only the Beatles. As for Ross, she would go on to even greater success as a solo artist and an actress. In fact, in 1976, *Billboard* magazine would honor her as the Female Entertainer of the Century.

Knocking on Motown's Door

Born on March 26, 1944, Diana Ross (born Diane; her name was changed due to a clerical error) grew up in the heart of Detroit, the second of six children. Diana was a strikingly pretty girl—and a bit of a tomboy. She loved to swim, run, dance, and sing, and she rarely sat still. "My family called me a wiggle tail," she recalled, "because I was a little skinny, wiry kid full of energy."[4]

While in high school, Ross, Ballard, Wilson, and Betty McGlowan tried hard to capture the attention of music insiders. Somehow, they seemed to find the right connections. Ballard's older sister dated Milton Jenkins, who managed a male group called the Primes (who would become the legendary Temptations). Jenkins decided to manage the four girls and call them the Primettes. Barbara Martin soon replaced McGlowan.

The Primettes played at parties to favorable reviews, but Diana had bigger dreams. In 1960, she summoned the courage to ask Smokey Robinson if he could get them an audition at Motown Records. The Detroit-based company, owned by Berry Gordy, was gaining the nickname "Hitsville, USA." (From 1961 to 1971, Motown would produce 110 Top Ten records.) Robinson got them an audition, and Gordy liked their sound, but he told them to come back when they finished high school. The Primettes were too impatient for that, however, so they kept returning to the studio. Every day.

The girls' persistence paid off, and in January 1961 Gordy signed them to a recording contract—even though they had yet to graduate. He hated the name Primettes, however, so they changed their name to the Supremes. Over the next two years, the girls recorded many songs without much success. Their first album, *Meet the Supremes* (1962), caused little stir. That same year, Martin left the group and Ross graduated from high school.

With their next album, *Where Did Our Love Go*, the Supremes seemed to make some headway. The second song released from the album, "When the Lovelight Starts Shining Through His Eyes," cracked the Top 40 on the pop charts. But it was the summer of 1964 when the Supremes' popularity took off. While they toured with Dick Clark's Caravan of Stars, their song "Where Did Our Love Go" was soaring up the charts. The Supremes were thrilled to hear their song on the bus's radio, and they couldn't believe that the kids in the audience knew the song when they performed it. By the end of the summer, "Where Did Our Love Go" had climbed to No. 1. "When the tour was over, we returned to Motown triumphant, with stars in our eyes," Ross wrote. "We were finally on our way."[5]

71

Belting Out the Hits

The Supremes were hardly a one hit wonder. The next two releases from the album, "Baby Love" and "Come See About Me," also shot to No. 1. While all three women

Diana Ross performed during the Divas With Heart concert in New York in 2008.

had shared lead vocals on earlier recordings, Ross sang the lead on the three No. 1s. Gordy preferred it that way, feeling that her sweet, feminine, honey-smooth voice would be more appealing to mainstream America.

With Ross as the focal point, the Supremes became Motown's main attraction. Two days after Christmas in 1964, they entertained millions on *The Ed Sullivan Show*. Their next two singles also rocketed to No. 1. "Stop! In the Name of Love" and "Back in My Arms Again" hit the top spot in the spring of 1965. This gave them five consecutive No. 1 records—all during the height of the Beatles' popularity.

By the end of 1966, three more Supremes songs topped the charts: "I Hear a Symphony," "You Can't Hurry Love," and the forceful "You Keep Me Hangin' On." After two No. 1s in early 1967, Florence Ballard left the group due largely to depression and alcoholism. Cindy Birdsong replaced her, and the new trio was renamed Diana Ross and the Supremes. But after two more No. 1 hits—"Love Child" and "Someday We'll Be Together"—Ross left the group. In early 1970, she launched a solo career.

Over the next few years, Diana Ross was pure magic. Her first solo single, "Reach Out and Touch," helped soothe a country ravaged by war and discontent. "Reach out and touch somebody's hand," she sang assuringly, "make this world a better place if you can." Later in 1970, she reached her zenith with "Ain't No Mountain High Enough." It sat atop the charts for three weeks and earned Ross a Grammy nomination.

In 1971, Ross married Robert Silberstein, gave birth to the first of her five children, and hosted her first TV special, *Diana!* She was a smash in *Lady Sings the Blues* (1972), winning an Oscar nomination for best actress for her portrayal of 1940s jazz singer Billie Holiday.

73

Career Highlights

* ❋ Diane Ernestine Earle Ross
* ❋ Born: March 26, 1944
* ❋ Hometown: Detroit, Michigan
* ❋ Genres: pop, soul, R&B, disco, jazz
* ❋ Skills: singer, actress, record producer
* ❋ First record: 1961
* ❋ Named "Female Entertainer of the Century" by *Billboard* magazine in 1976
* ❋ Charted twelve No. 1 singles with the Supremes
* ❋ Became the first solo artist with six No. 1 songs
* ❋ Has recorded fifty-seven studio albums

The movie's soundtrack hit No. 1 in 1973, as did Ross's single "Touch Me in the Morning." The next decade brought four more No. 1 singles, and two more movies (*Mahogany* and *The Wiz*). She cohosted the Academy Awards, sang at the Super Bowl, and attracted four hundred thousand fans to a free concert in New York's Central Park.

Ross has always brought a comforting, almost healing quality to her performances. This was never more evident than on September 21, 2001. It was the New York Mets' first game after the 9/11 attacks on sites including New

York's World Trade Center. Ross touched hearts with her rendition of "God Bless America." "Everybody who was standing, watching was crying," said Mets general manager Steve Phillips. "She was walking around, she had choirs out there, she was singing and touching the choirs' faces—oh, unbelievable."[6]

Well into her sixties, Ross continued to sing at various events. She performed on tour in 2004, and released an album of new material three years later. She has written two autobiographies. She also has earned a pair of stars on the Hollywood Walk of Fame—one as a solo artist and one for the Supremes. To top it off, she even earned a spot in the *Guinness Book of World Records*. No woman in history has equaled her eighteen No. 1 singles—six solo and twelve with the Supremes. In 1993, Guinness labeled her the most successful female singer of all time.

Not bad for a kid who just wanted to make a record.

Diana Ross Timeline

January 15, 1961—The Supremes sign with Motown Records.

August 22, 1964—"Where Did Our Love Go" becomes the first of twelve Supremes singles to hit No. 1 on the pop charts.

October 31, 1964—"Baby Love" goes to No. 1.

June 12, 1965—"Back in My Arms Again" is the Supremes' fifth consecutive No. 1 record.

October 22, 1966—*The Supremes A' Go-Go* becomes the group's first No. 1 album in the United States.

December 27, 1969—"Someday We'll Be Together" is the Supremes' last No. 1 single.

September 19, 1970—Sees her first solo single, "Ain't No Mountain High Enough," rise to No. 1.

October 17, 1972—Release of *Lady Sings the Blues*, her movie premiere.

March 6, 1977—*An Evening With Diana Ross* airs on NBC.

September 6, 1980—"Upside Down," a disco song, hits No. 1.

August 15, 1981—"Endless Love," a duet with Lionel Richie, rests at No. 1 for the first of nine weeks.

July 21, 1983—Performs in front of four hundred thousand fans in Central Park in New York.

May 16, 2007—Receives BET (Black Entertainment Television) Lifetime Achievement Award.

November 3, 2007—The album *I Love You* reaches the top 40.

December 3, 2007—Receives Kennedy Center Honor.

May 15, 2010—Ross's *More Today Than Yesterday: The Greatest Hits Tour* begins.

Stevie Wonder posing
for photos

Chapter 8

Stevie Wonder

Lula Mae Hardaway worried so much about her blind son. It pained her to go to work and leave him alone with his brothers. She fretted that he would bump into things and hurt himself. It broke her heart that he spent his life in total darkness. Stevie felt bad, too—not for himself, but for his mom.

"I know it used to worry my mother," he said, "and I know she prayed for me to have sight someday, and so finally I just told her that I was happy being blind, and I thought it was a gift from God, and I think she felt better after that."[1]

Throughout his life, Stevie Wonder has made the whole world feel better. In his 1963 hit song "Fingertips (Pt. 2)," the young, blind singer urged listeners to "clap your hands just a little bit louder." His fans have been doing so ever since. His music inspires and excites—makes people clap, dance, and sing along. It's hard for listeners to classify his music as R&B, funk, soul, or rock 'n' roll. But it is distinctly Stevie. He has given us such musical treats as "Superstition" and "Signed, Sealed, Delivered,

79

I'm Yours." Along the way, he has won twenty-five Grammy Awards—more than any other solo artist.

"That Kid's a Wonder!"

Stevland Hardaway Judkins was born in Saginaw, Michigan, on May 13, 1950. It would have been a happy day except that Stevie was supposed to be born in mid-June. The premature baby was placed in an incubator, where he received too much oxygen. That caused a condition called retrolental fibroplasias, which made him go blind. Later in life, Wonder took a positive approach to the ordeal. "I was premature by one full month," he said. "But a girl who was born on the same day that I was was also put into the incubator, and she died. I personally think that I'm lucky to be alive."[2]

Early in life, Stevie didn't know what "blind" and "sight" meant. He figured that everyone lived like he did. His older brothers, Calvin and Milton, didn't fully understand Stevie's condition, either. They thought that he just needed more light to see. One day, they decided to provide more light for Stevie by igniting a fire in a garbage can. They almost burned the house down.

For Stevie, sound became his way of exploring the world. He identified birds by their chirps and trees by the way their leaves rustled in the wind. Voices and musical instruments also fascinated him. As a young boy, he took his transistor radio to bed and listened to music under the sheets. He loved to mimic voices, sing, and bang on toy drums.

In 1954, Stevie's mother, having left his father, moved the family to Detroit, Michigan. The family was poor and couldn't afford to buy instruments for Stevie. But people in the community knew how much he loved music, and they opened their hearts to him. The Detroit Lions Club, which held a Christmas party for the blind children at Stevie's school when he was in first grade, gave him a drum set. His barber offered him a harmonica, and a woman in the neighborhood donated a piano that she no longer wanted.

Stevie learned to play all these instruments, but his voice is what impressed his neighbors. His strong, beautiful vocals filled his church every Sunday. He sang on front porches, sometimes imitating his idol, Ray Charles (who was also blind). He even formed a duo, "Steve and John," with his best friend, John Glover.

When Stevie was ten years old, John arranged for his cousin, Ronnie White of the Miracles, to listen to Stevie sing. White was so impressed that he brought Stevie to Motown Records. There, he wowed Motown president Berry Gordy as well as Gordy's sister, Esther. "Boy!" she exclaimed. "That kid's a wonder."[3] The nickname stuck. Gordy signed him to a contract, and he became known professionally as Little Stevie Wonder.

Every day after school, Stevie hung out at the Motown studios. He sang, played instruments, and listened to the extraordinary musical artists who cut records for Motown. Stevie's fellow students, largely out of jealousy, told him he would never make it in music. By age thirteen, he had proved them wrong. "Fingertips (Pt. 2)," on which Stevie sang and played the bongos and harmonica, became the No 1. song in the country.

Up through 1971, Wonder recorded thirteen Top Ten hits for Motown. Some of them are still played daily on American radio stations: "Uptight (Everything's Alright)," "For Once in My Life," "My Cherie Amour," and "Yester-Me, Yester-You, Yesterday." During this period, Stevie's mother cowrote two of his all-time greatest

Stevie Wonder performing at the Hole in the Wall Camps benefit concert in New York in 2010

hits—"I Was Made to Love Her" and "Signed, Sealed, Delivered, I'm Yours."

And the Grammys Go to . . .

Beginning in 1971, Wonder was granted more artistic control of his music. He made the most of it. From 1972 to 1976, he produced five extraordinary and influential albums. Three of them, in fact, would be included among *Rolling Stone*'s list of the top 100 albums of all time. First came *Music of My Mind*, on which Wonder plays nearly all the instruments. He followed up with *Talking Book*, in which he displays his mastery of the clavinet (an electrophonic keyboard). The album features two No. 1 hits: the soft ballad "You Are the Sunshine of My Life" and the funky "Superstition," which won a Grammy for best song of the year.

Wonder's next masterpiece, *Innervisions*, won a Grammy Award for album of the year. The first disc included the Grammy-winning song "Living for the City," which reflects the hardships of a poor African-American family. "His father works some days for fourteen hours," Wonder sings, "and you can bet he barely makes a dollar."

On August 6, 1973, Wonder suffered a serious head injury in an auto accident. He lay in a coma for four days. Although he permanently lost his sense of smell, his musical capacities were unaffected. His next album, *Fulfillingness' First Finale*, won another Grammy for album of the year. In 1976, Wonder reached even greater heights with the double album *Songs in the Key of Life*. This ambitious effort featured a bit of everything: funk, rock, jazz, soul, swing, Latin, gospel...even Hare Krishna chants. The singles "I Wish" and "Sir Duke" topped the charts. Wonder was so popular at the time that his album debuted at No. 1—a first for an American artist.

Career Highlights

❋ Stevland Hardaway Judkins

❋ Born: May 13, 1950

❋ Hometown: Saginaw, Michigan

❋ Genres: R&B, funk, soul, pop

❋ Skills: singer, songwriter, multi-instrumentalist, record producer

❋ First record: 1961

❋ Has won twenty-five Grammy Awards (most for a solo artist)

❋ Has scored nine No. 1 hits

❋ Has sold more than 100 million albums

❋ Won an Oscar for best song

After 1976, Wonder released albums sporadically. Some were highly experimental, especially the eccentric *Journey Through the Secret Life of Plants* (1979). Yet he remained a hit maker in the 1980s, reaching No. 1 with four famous singles. First came "Ebony and Ivory," a duet with Paul McCartney about racial harmony. The mid-1980s brought the chart toppers "I Just Called to Say I Love You," "Part-Time Lover," and "That's What Friends Are For" (with Dionne Warwick, Elton John, and Gladys Knight).

For much of his life, Wonder has been involved in activism and politics. He lobbied for gun control, rallied against apartheid in South Africa, and pushed for the establishment of a national holiday for Martin Luther King, Jr. He also was featured on a poster for Mothers Against Drunk Driving (MADD). The words below his picture read: "Before I ride with a drunk, I'll drive myself."[4]

Over the years, Wonder has been showered with awards, applause, and adulations. He cannot walk in public without strangers—people he'll never see—shouting, "I love you!" The joy that radiates from Stevie always comes back to him—and he loves it. "I'm still feeling new and amazed by the world I live in," he said in 1995. "I was in the Hard Rock Cafe in Tokyo last week, and they started playing my records, and I started crying, crying like a little kid, thinking how God has blessed me with all these songs."[5]

Stevie Wonder Timeline

August 10, 1963—At thirteen years old, tops the pop chart with "Fingertips (Pt. 2)."

October 27, 1972—Releases *Talking Book*, which includes the No. 1 hits "You Are the Sunshine of My Life" and the funky "Superstition."

August 3, 1973—Releases *Innervisions*, which will win a Grammy Award for album of the year.

August 6, 1973—Is critically injured in an auto accident.

March 2, 1974—Wins five Grammy Awards.

July 22, 1974—Releases *Fulfillingness' First Finale*, which will hit No. 1 and win a Grammy for album of the year.

March 1, 1975—Wins four more Grammy Awards.

September 28, 1976—Releases *Songs in the Key of Life*, which debuts at No. 1. and includes the No. 1 hits "I Wish" and "Sir Duke."

March 29, 1982—Releases the international hit "Ebony and Ivory," a duet with Paul McCartney.

October 13, 1984— "I Just Called to Say I Love You" rises to No. 1.

1985—"Part-Time Lover", and "That's What Friends Are For" (with Dionne Warwick, Elton John, and Gladys Knight), hit No. 1.

January 18, 1989—Inducted into the Rock and Roll Hall of Fame.

November 1999—Receives Kennedy Center Honor.

May 6, 2002—Receives the George and Ira Gershwin Lifetime Achievement Award.

October 18, 2005—Releases *A Time to Love*.

2009—Is recognized with the Second Library of Congress Gershwin Prize for Popular Song.

Prince performing
in the United Kingdom
in 2011

Chapter 9

Prince

It's okay to be a little bit different, as Prince can attest. Growing up in conservative Minneapolis, Minnesota, he was often ridiculed because of how he looked and acted. Prince and his "lunatic" friends (as he called them) "took a lot of heat all the time," he said. "People would say something about our clothes or the way we looked or who we were with, and we'd end up fighting."[1]

Short for his age, Prince also was the product of a broken home. His parents divorced when he was seven, and he clashed so much with his stepfather that he couldn't bear to live with him. "I ran away from home when I was twelve," he said. "I've changed address in Minneapolis thirty-two times, and there was a great deal of loneliness."[2] Prince lived for a while with his father, then with a married couple in his neighborhood. Fortunately, he found an outlet for all the emotions that swirled within him: music.

Through his lyrics and instruments, he could express his loneliness, love, anger, and desire. For Prince, music became his breath of life. He formed a band in junior high school and kept on playing. He learned to play more than two dozen instruments, and he sang, composed, arranged, and produced his albums. He has written hundreds of songs, for himself and others. His live performances have been outrageous and spectacular. He has won Grammys, an Oscar, and a Golden Globe Award, as well as international acclaim.

Raved Bill Adler in *Rolling Stone*:

> As a songwriter...he ranks with Lennon and McCartney, Bob Dylan, and Smokey Robinson; as a guitarist, with Hendrix and Steve Cropper. He was the most influential record producer and arranger of the '80s....No artist has swung as fluently from style to style (hard rock, stripped-down funk, jazzy show tunes, intoxicated balladry, kid-pop, dance raunch), and only [James Brown] has put on more incendiary live shows.[3]

Marching to His Own Drum

On June 7, 1958, Mattie Shaw gave birth to the future legend. He was named Prince Rogers Nelson after the jazz band Prince Rogers Trio, of which his father, John Nelson, was a member. As an adolescent, Prince performed in his own band, Grand Central. The group evolved into Champagne, and the members began to write their own material. However, they broke up before making any recordings.

Prince proved to be a band unto himself. After signing a record contract with Warner Bros. at age eighteen, he released his first album, *For You*, in 1978. Prince wrote the music and played all twenty-seven instruments! He churned out an album a year through 1981. His music was classified as R&B, dance, and funk—as well as ingenious and provocative. But mainstream society wasn't ready for him. When he opened for the Rolling

Stones in Los Angeles, he was booed off the stage because of his risqué outfit.

But in 1982, Prince self-produced a double album, *1999*, that was ripe for the masses. The highly charged music appealed to fans of disco and new wave, of black funk and white rock. Teens danced to the songs at parties and clubs, and millions sang along to the irresistible lyrics. He sings in the title track: "They say two thousand zero, zero, party over, Oops, out of time! So tonight I'm gonna party like it's 1999." The album's other huge hits, "Little Red Corvette" and "Delirious," ensured Prince's place among pop's royal hierarchy.

Prince Rains

In 1984, Prince and the Revolution took the nation by storm with the album *Purple Rain*. During the decade, only Michael Jackson's *Thriller*, Madonna's *Like a Virgin*, and Bruce Springsteen's *Born in the U.S.A.* could compare to this monumental effort. The complicated arrangements included guitars, keyboards, synthesizers, drum machines, and other instruments. The result was a wondrous explosion of sound, punctuated by Prince's passionate vocals.

Purple Rain sat at No. 1 on *Billboard*'s album chart for twenty-four consecutive weeks. Thirteen million copies of the album were sold in the United States alone. The cuts "When Doves Cry" and "Let's Go Crazy" rocketed to No. 1 on the pop charts. The title track hit No. 2, and "I Would Die 4 U" reached No. 8. The album earned Prince three Grammy Awards, and in 1993 *Time* magazine would rate it the No. 15 album of all time.

In addition, the accompanying film of the same name became a box-office smash, grossing close to $100 million. The endlessly talented Prince starred in the film as an

91

Prince during a 1985 concert

anguished Minneapolis musician named "The Kid." The film earned him an Academy Award for best soundtrack.

A voracious worker, Prince released an album of psychedelic soul in 1985. It was called *Around the World in a Day*, and it too shot to No. 1. From coast to coast, kids sang "Raspberry Beret" ("raaaaz-berry beret"), which hit No. 2 on the singles chart. A year later, Prince directed his first film, *Under the Cherry Moon*. He would direct two more movies, *Sign 'O' the Times* (1988) and *Graffiti Bridge* (1990). He starred in and provided the music for each of the films. The soundtrack for *Under the Cherry Moon*, titled *Parade*, included his third No. 1 single, "Kiss."

A deep source of music, Prince has written numerous songs for fellow artists. During the same week that "Kiss" hit No. 1, "Manic Monday"—which Prince wrote for the Bangles—sat at No. 2. In 1990, singer Sinead O'Connor rode Prince's "Nothing Compares 2 U" to international superstardom.

In 1987, Prince opened Paisley Park, an enormous multimedia production facility in Minneapolis. He also released the double album *Sign 'O' the Times*, which the Rock and Roll Hall of Fame calls "Prince's most musically expansive and lyrically incisive album." The cut "U Got the Look" hit No. 2 on the pop charts. Prince's soundtrack for the 1989 blockbuster movie *Batman* rose to the top of the charts. So too did the single "Batdance."

Backed by the New Power Generation, Prince produced the successful *Diamonds and Pearls* album in 1991. In 1992, he signed a Warner Bros. Records contract worth tens of millions of dollars. The first music Prince produced under this contract greatly displeased Warner executives, who had tried to guide him to a more mainstream style to protect their investment. As a result, Prince simply stopped writing music under this contract.

Career Highlights

❉ Prince Rogers Nelson

❉ Born: June 7, 1958

❉ Hometown: Minneapolis, Minnesota

❉ Genres: pop, funk, rock, R&B

❉ Skills: singer, songwriter, multi-instrumentalist, record producer, actor

❉ First record: 1978

❉ Has sold more than eighty million albums

❉ *Purple Rain* sold more than thirteen million copies

❉ Has won multiple Grammy Awards, a Golden Globe Award, and an Oscar

❉ Has starred in three films, directing two of them

However, wishing to continue making music his own way, Prince changed his name to a self-made "love symbol" and called himself "the artist formerly known as Prince."

For the rest of the decade, Prince produced critically acclaimed music—and lots of it. From 1996 to 1998, he released the three-disc *Emancipation* and the single CDs *Chaos and Disorder* and *Newpower Soul*. In 1998, he also issued a three-disc set of previously unreleased songs called *Crystal Ball*. That's eight CDs in three years!

In 2000, after being freed from his obligations to Warner Bros., he became known as Prince again. His 2001 album, *The Rainbow Children*, celebrated his conversion to the Jehovah's Witnesses. By 2007, he had released fifteen albums in the 21st century. He also embraced mainstream outlets. His "Song of the Heart" for the 2006 animated film *Happy Feet* earned him a Golden Globe Award for best original song. And in February 2007, he performed before an international audience during halftime of the Super Bowl.

No one laughs at Prince anymore. He earns only respect and praise as one of the greatest pop music artists of our time.

Prince Timeline

April 7, 1978—Releases his first album, *For You*.

October 27, 1982—Releases his breakthrough album, *1999*, which features the hits "1999" and "Little Red Corvette."

August 4, 1984—The blockbuster album *Purple Rain* hits No. 1 for the first of twenty-four consecutive weeks. The cuts "Let's Go Crazy" and "When Doves Cry" will hit No. 1 on the pop chart.

July 27, 1984—The movie *Purple Rain* opens in theaters. Prince stars in the movie and will win an Oscar for his music.

April 22, 1985—Releases *Around the World in a Day*, which will ascend to No. 1 on the album chart.

July 2, 1986—Directs his first movie, *Under the Cherry Moon*.

March 31, 1987—Releases the acclaimed album *Sign 'O' the Times*.

June 20, 1989—The soundtrack for *Batman*, featuring the No. 1 song "Batdance," reaches No. 1 on the album chart.

October 1, 1991—Releases *Diamonds and Pearls*, which includes the No. 1 song "Cream."

1993—Changes his name to the "love symbol."

March 15, 2004—Is inducted into the Rock and Roll Hall of Fame.

February 13, 2005—Receives two Grammy Awards for his vocal performances on the album *Musicology*.

2009, 2010—Explores new ways to distribute his music. The three-CD set *LOtUSFLOW3R* is sold exclusively through Target stores; *20Ten* is distributed free with several European publications.

Chapter Notes

Introduction

1. Kevin Chappell, "How Blacks Invented Rock and Roll," *Ebony*, January 1997, <http://findarticles.com/p/articles/mi_m1077/is_9_56/ai_76285243> (June 18, 2008).
2. Ibid.
3. "Our Music," 1960 Sailors Association, Inc., n.d., <http://www.1960sailors.net/05_our_music.htm> (June 20, 2008).
4. Chappell.
5. Ibid.
6. "Ray Charles Quotes," BrainyQuote, n.d., <http://www.brainyquote.com/quotes/authors/r/ray_charles.html> (June 21, 2008).
7. "Lady Soul Singing It Like It Is," *Time*, June 28, 1968, <http://www.time.com/time/magazine/article/0,9171,841340-5,00.html> (June 18, 2008).

Chapter 1
Chuck Berry

1. "About Chuck Berry," The Official Site of Chuck Berry, n.d., <http://www.chuckberry.com/about/quotes.htm> (April 24, 2008).
2. "Chuck Berry," Rock and Roll Hall of Fame, n.d., <http://www.rockhall.com/inductee/chuck-berry> (April 25, 2008).
3. David P. Szatmary, *Rockin' in Time: A Social History of Rock-and-Roll* (Upper Saddle River, N.J.: Prentice-Hall, 1987), p. 21.
4. Ibid., p. 18.
5. "About Chuck Berry," The Official Site of Chuck Berry, n.d., <http://www.chuckberry.com/about/quotes.htm> (April 24, 2008).
6. Ibid.
7. Ibid.

Chapter 2
Ray Charles

1. "Autobiography," Ray Charles, n.d., <http://www
   .raycharles.com/the_man_autobiography.html> (May
   4, 2008).
2. Ibid.
3. Ibid.
4. "Recording With Ray Charles: Artists Quotes," Ray
   Charles, n.d., <http://www.raycharles.com/the_legacy_
   remembering_ray.html> (May 4, 2008).
5. Ray Charles and David Ritz, *Brother Ray* (New York:
   DaCapo Press, 2003), p. 45.
6. "Recording With Ray Charles: Artists Quotes," Ray
   Charles, n.d., <http://www.raycharles.com/the_legacy_
   remembering_ray.html> (May 4, 2008).

Chapter 3
Little Richard

1. Glenn C. Altschuler, *All Shook Up: How Rock 'n' Roll
   Changed America* (New York: Oxford University Press,
   2003), p. 58.
2. Wayne Robins, *A Brief History of Rock, Off the Record* (New
   York: Taylor and Francis Group, 2008), p. 39.
3. Altschuler, p. 58.
4. Ibid, p. 162.
5. Charles White, *The Life and Times of Little Richard:
   The Quasar of Rock* (New York: Da Capo Press, 1994),
   pp. 91-92. <http://books.google.com/books?id=vS
   zzpbNXURoC&pg=PA91&lpg=PA91&dq=%22It+lo
   oked+as+though+the+big+ball+of+fire+came+
   &source=web&ots=K2e8FpK8CA&sig=vGePUvVkT
   BnOLwu6an1TOfndSZM&hl=en&sa=X&oi=book_
   result&resnum=1&ct=result> (December 15, 2008).
6. Charles Shaar Murray, *Crosstown Traffic: Jimi Hendrix
   and the Post-War Rock 'n' Roll Revolution* (New York:
   Macmillan, 1991), p. 39. <http://books.google.com/

books?id=CiWtlIxnQ6gC&pg=PA39&lpg=PA39&dq=%2
2I+want+to+do+with+my+guitar+what+Little+Rich
ard+does+with+his+voice.&source=web&ots=D6FYKK
kl2M&sig=4Uku5iuxVPcvF9qKUX4CNFiuDRA&hl=en>

7. "Mojo (magazine)," Wikipedia, n.d., <http://
en.wikipedia.org/wiki/Mojo_(magazine)> (April 27,
2008).

Chapter 4

James Brown

1. "James Brown Quotes," BrainyQuote, n.d., <http://
www.brainyquote.com/quotes/authors/j/james_brown
.html> (May 1, 2008).

2. "James Brown," Rock and Roll Hall of Fame, n.d.,
<http://www.rockhall.com/inductee/james-brown>
(May 1, 2008).

3. "James Brown Quotes," BrainyQuote, n.d., <http://
www.brainyquote.com/quotes/authors/j/james_brown
.html> (May 1, 2008).

4. Robert Dimery, ed. *1001 Albums You Must Hear Before You
Die* (New York: Quintet Publishing, 2005), p. 63.

5. "James Brown, the 'Godfather of Soul,' dies at 73," CNN,
December 25, 2006, <http://www.cnn.com/2006/
SHOWBIZ/Music/12/25/obit.brown/index.html> (May
2, 2008).

6. James Brown, Bruce Tucker, Al Sharpton, *James Brown:
The Godfather of Soul* (New York: Avalon Press, 2002), p.
158.

7. Kip Grosenick, "James Brown's Got a Brand New Bag:
School Violence," CNN, May 22, 2001, <http://archives
.cnn.com/2001/SHOWBIZ/Music/05/22/james.brown/
index.html> (May 2, 2008).

8. "James Brown, the 'Godfather of Soul,' dies at 73," CNN,
December 25, 2006, <http://www.cnn.com/2006/
SHOWBIZ/Music/12/25/obit.brown/index.html> (May
2, 2008).

Chapter 5
Aretha Franklin

1. Judith Tick, ed., *Music in the USA* (New York: Oxford University Press, 2008), p. 615.
2. Jon Pareles, "Review/Pop; Aretha Franklin, Body and Soul," *New York Times*, July 8, 1989, <http://query.nytimes.com/gst/fullpage.html?res=950DE6D91039F93BA35754C0A96F948260> (May 13, 2008).
3. "Lady Soul Singing It Like It Is," *Time*, June 28, 1968, <http://www.time.com/time/magazine/article/0,9171,841340-2,00.html> (May 13, 2008).
4. Ibid.
5. "Aretha Franklin," Rock and Roll Hall of Fame, n.d., <http://www.rockhall.com/inductee/aretha-franklin> (May 14, 2008).
6. "Lady Soul Singing It Like It Is," *Time*, June 28, 1968, <http://www.time.com/time/magazine/article/0,9171,841340-4,00.html> (May 13, 2008).

Chapter 6
Jimi Hendrix

1. "Jimi Hendrix—Wild Thing Live at Monterey," YouTube, July 13, 2007, <http://www.youtube.com/watch?v=hfPgj4bviKY> (May 23, 2008). Quote begins at 2:03 of video.
2. Chris Welch, *Hendrix: A Biography* (London: Omnibus Press, 1982), p. 16.<http://books.google.com/books?id=JCTqqzA60UIC&pg=PA16&lpg=PA16&dq=%22mean+I+like+to+play+it+every+night.&source=web&ots=SvyQfgrSZ-&sig=TFGgNzKdQShdhhno_ur0LF3UyQo&hl=en> (May 23, 2008).
3. "The Jimi Hendrix Experience," Rock and Roll Hall of Fame, n.d., <http://www.rockhall.com/inductee/the-jimi-hendrix-experience> (May 24, 2008).
4. Wayne Robins, *A Brief History of Rock, Off the Record* (New York: Taylor and Francis Group, 2008), p. 132.

101

5. David P. Szatmary, *Rockin' in Time: A Social History of Rock-and-Roll* (Upper Saddle River, N.J.: Prentice-Hall, 1987) p. 176.
6. Ibid.
7. Reebee Garofalo, *Rockin' Out: Popular Music in the USA* (Boston: University of Massachusetts, 1997), p. 225.
8. "Jimi Hendrix Quotes," BrainyQuote, n.d., <http://www.brainyquote.com/quotes/authors/j/jimi_hendrix.html> (May 25, 2008).

Chapter 7
Diana Ross

1. Diana Ross, *Secrets of a Sparrow* (New York: Villard Books, 1993), p. 90.
2. Ibid., p. 91.
3. Ibid., p. 93.
4. "Diana Ross Quotes," BrainyQuote, n.d., <http://www.brainyquote.com/quotes/authors/d/diana_ross.html> (May 9, 2008).
5. Ross, *Secrets of a Sparrow*, p. 118.
6. "Time Pieces," A Diana Ross Tribute, n.d., <http://www.diana-web.com> (May 10, 2008).

Chapter 8
Stevie Wonder

1. James Haskins, *The Story of Stevie Wonder* (New York: Lothrop, Lee & Shepard Company, 1976), p. 14.
2. Ibid., p. 10.
3. Robert E. Johnson, "Berry Gordy's Book, 'To Be Loved,' Tells How He Shaped Lives of Motown Stars," *Jet*, November 21, 1994, <http://findarticles.com/p/articles/mi_m1355/is_n3_v87/ai_15969366> (May 17, 2008).
4. "Stevie Wonder Biography," Brief Biographies, n.d., <http://biography.jrank.org/pages/2835/Wonder-Stevie.html> (May 17, 2008).

5. Ibid.

Chapter 9
Prince

1. Bill Adler, "Will the Little Girls Understand?" *Rolling Stone*, February 19, 1981, <http://princetext.tripod .com/i_stone81.html> (May 28, 2008).
2. Ibid.
3. *Rolling Stone Album Guide* (New York: Simon & Schuster, 2004), p. 655.

Glossary

apartheid—A policy of racial separation that was maintained in South Africa from 1948 to 1994.

arrangement—A piece of music that has been adapted for performance by a particular set of instruments and/or voices.

backbeat—A rhythm that emphasizes the second and fourth beats of every four-beat measure: one-*two*-three-*four*.

ballad—A song that tells a story.

beat—A basic time unit of a musical piece.

boogie-woogie music—A style of piano-playing blues.

calypso music—A style of music from the West Indies characterized by lively rhythm, steel drums, and humorous lyrics.

chitlin circuit—Nightclubs where black musicians were welcome to play during racial segragation.

civil rights movement—An effort to bring about racial and gender equality during the 1960s.

country music—A style of folk music that is played with stringed instruments; associated with the American South.

country and western music—Like country music only with a tendency toward steel guitars and big bands; a combination of music from the American South, Southwest, and West.

cover version—A performance or recording by one artist of another artist's song; it may be in a similar or different style.

demo tape—An audio tape recording of a musician's songs, often using simple arrangements, submitted for audition purposes; MP3s or CDs are used today.

disco music—Popular dance (discotheque) music that thrived during the 1970s; melodic with pronounced bass and a regular beat.

funk music—Derived from R&B, jazz, and soul music in the late 1960s; emphasizes a steady rhythm with drumlike vocals and punchy horns.

genre (ZHAN-ruh)—A style of music, identified by its typical melodies, rhythms, harmonies, and/or lyrics.

glaucoma—A medical disorder characterized by excessive fluid pressure in the eyeball; can cause vision loss or blindness.

gospel music—Christian-themed music dominated by strong vocals; popularized by African Americans in the 20th century.

Grammy Awards—An annual award ceremony by the National Academy of

105

Recording Arts and Sciences of the United States; recognizes outstanding achievements in the music industry.

hillbilly music—Country music that originated in the mountainous regions of the southern United States.

jazz music—Rhythmic music characterized by improvisation and strong expressions of emotion; originated in the American South.

Latin music—A diverse range of music from Latin American countries.

melody—A succession of notes that forms a distinctive sequence.

octave—A full series of eight notes on the musical scale.

pop music—Popular music of the era.

rap music—A genre of African-American music that emerged in the 1980s; rhyming lyrics are chanted to a musical accompaniment.

rhythm and blues (R&B) music—Popular music that features a blues theme and a strong rhythm.

rhythm section—A group of instruments (in an orchestra or band) that provides the harmonic and rhythmic structure.

riff—A melodic pattern repeated many times in a piece of music.

rock 'n' roll music—High-energy, popular music that emerged in the 1950s; features a strong backbeat and (often) electric guitar.

single—A 7-inch, 45-rpm vinyl record featuring the promoted song (the A side) and a second recording on the B side.

soul music—Expressive African-American music that emerged in the 1960s; a combination of gospel and R&B.

spirituals—Religious folk songs of African Americans; characterized by strong emotions.

swing music—A style of jazz music played by big bands; popular in the 1930s.

transistor radio—A small, portable radio.

Further Reading

Beyer, Mark. *Rock & Roll Hall of Famers: Stevie Wonder*. New York: Rosen Publishing Group, 2002.

Fandel, Jennifer. *James Brown*. Chicago: Heinemann-Raintree, 2003.

Kirby, David. *Little Richard: The Birth of Rock 'n' Roll*. New York: Continuum, 2009.

Robins, Wayne. *A Brief History of Rock, Off the Record*. New York: Routledge, 2008.

Rolling Stone: The Decades of Rock & Roll. San Francisco: Chronicle Books, 2001.

The Rolling Stone Illustrated History of Rock & Roll. New York: Random House, 1992.

Ross, Diana. *Secrets of a Sparrow*. New York: Villard Books, 1993.

Sgolla, Lisa Jo. *Rock 'n' Roll Dances of the 1950s*. Santa Barbara, CA: Greenwood, 2011.

Sloate, Susan. *Ray Charles: Young Musician*. New York: Aladdin Paperbacks, 2007.

Wagner, Heather Lehr. *Aretha Franklin: Singer*. Philadelphia: Chelsea House Publications, 2010.

Werner, Craig Hansen. *Higher Ground: Stevie Wonder, Aretha Franklin, Curtis Mayfield, and the Rise and Fall of American Soul*. New York: Crown Publishers, 2004.

Internet Addresses

The Rock and Roll Hall of Fame and Museum
<http://rockhall.com>

Rolling Stone Music Artists Page
<http://www.rollingstone.com/music/artists>

Soulmusic.com
<http://www.soulmusic.com>

Index